Advance Praise for *Dervish*

"In his debut collection *Dervish*, Gerard Wozek shares generously of an open, attentive heart and a wide-ranging vision. In these pages, find potent spells, incantations, recitations, and prayers that summon forth the poet's sharp determination to move beyond mere survival into a fiery thriving, even—perhaps, especially—in the midst of loss and devastation. By Jove, these poems shimmer."

—Gerry Gomez Pearlberg, author of *Mr. Bluebird*

"The farflung geography of Gerard Wozek's *Dervish* suggests a journey, but the real landscape here is the untamed territory of the open heart. This restless gay man's garden of verses is as innocent and worldly as a dried bouquet hanging behind the counter of a café in Prague. Heartfelt, graceful, eloquent and erudite, Gerard Wozek's poems are compelling and moving —redolent, perhaps, of some future nostalgia for lessons learned long ago, in youth."

—Michael Lassell, author of *A Flame for the Touch That Matters*

"Gerard Wozek looks for miracles in everyday moments, chance encounters, trysts and rituals. Whether set in Paris, Vienna, LaSpezia, Mexico City, or Saugatuck, these poems written 'in remembrance of seraphs' celebrate a gritty reverence for the body as they draw on pagan and Christian influences. In Wozek's poems, gay sensibility and spiritual longing are one and the same."

—Karen Lee Osborne, author of the novels *Carlyle Simpson* and *Hawkwings*, and the prose poem chapbook *Survival*

"'Hunger is instructional', says Gerard Wozek, and in *Dervish* that same hunger makes the world luminous. Whether describing a Viennese coffeehouse, a beach by Lake Michigan, an erotic bookstore, or a Parisian cemetery, Wozek captures the unceasing, insatiable whirl of the body's appetites and the music Eros lends to existence. Reading *Dervish*, we join the speaker's attempts to 'trust this pulse, this sweat,' to 'keep [touch] holy,' to carve out a 'destiny / that matters.'"

—Jeff Mann, author of *Flint Shards from Sussex*

Dervish

Gerard Wozek

Gival Press

Arlington, Virginia

DERVISH. Copyright © 2001 by Gerard Wozek.

All Rights Reserved. Printed in the United States of America. With the exception of brief quotations in the body of critical articles or reviews, no part of the book may be reproduced or transmitted in any form or by any means, graphic, electronic, or mechanical, including photocopying, recording, taping, or by any information storage or retrieval system, without the permission in writing from the publisher.

Published by Gival Press, an imprint of Gival Press, LLC.
For information please write:
Gival Press, LLC, P. O. Box 3812, Arlington, Virginia 22203.
Website: givalpress.com

First Edition
ISBN 1-928589-11-1
Library of Congress Card Number 2001089881

Format and design by Ken Schellenberg
Cover art "Swallow Song" © 2001 by Mary Russell
Back cover photograph by Anna E. Dassonville

Acknowledgements

Prefatory quotation from *BREATHING THE WATER* by Denise Levertov., Copyright 1987 by Denise Levertov. Reprinted by permission of New Directions Publishing Corp.

The poems in this book have appeared in different versions in the following publications:

Bay Windows: Confessing Sins, (June, 1996)
Chiron Review: Ritual for Letting Go, (Issue #50, Spring 1997)
Gayplace Magazine: Heaven of the Fixed Stars, The Hula Room on Highway B, (October, 1997)
Gents, Bad Boys, and Barbarians (Alyson Press): The Berdache's Kiss, (1995)
Off the Rocks: Troubadours of Fire, (Volume 6, 1991)
Pif Magazine: Manifest, (Number 18, November, 1998)
Queer Dog (Cleis Press): Side Show, (1997)
River Oak Review: Temple of Wings, (Issue 14, Spring 2001)
Spillway: Tiger's Eye, (Number 7, Spring/Summer 1998)

Contents

Temple of Wings 9
My Roman Spring 11
Fakir 14
Crèche 15
Cavafy's Bones 16
Troll Cat's Truck Stop 17
The Hula Room
    on Highway B 18
Saugatuck:
    Ode to the Dunes 19
When you wake up after sleeping 21
Side Show 22
Manifest 23
Spell for Changing Bodies 25
Pilgrimage 26
Dervish 30
Vienna 32
Gellert Hotel Sauna 36
At Sitges 37
Song for Distingue Lovers 38
A Calendar from Krakow 39
Lucia di Lammermoor 40
Le Mal du Pays 41
Tiger's Eye 42
Daylight 44
Elk Song 45
Ritual for Letting Go 46

Rumi 47
Heaven of the Fixed Stars 48
Troubadours of Fire 49
Confessing Sins 51
Ice Elegy (after Takamura Kotaro) 52
The Berdache's Kiss 53
Say Goodbye 54
Shaman 56

"and nothing was burning,
nothing but I, as that hand of fire
touched my lips and scorched my tongue
and pulled my voice
into the ring of the dance."

by Denise Levertov
from *BREATHING THE WATER*

Temple of Wings

What is permanent?
That mountain sloped
toward the lake,
our bucolic sun waving a truce
through lavender smog?
I play patty-cake with a sea anemone
as the tide hoards up sand bridges.
I'm forgetting again: blights, viruses,
the enemies of song.

I move into open spaces
the way a spark devours a path
of acetylene, burning up old selves,
losing faithlessness,
rendering shyness to ash.
What will finally save us from ourselves?
Giotto's stalwart cherubs marking time
on chapel frescos, music that lopes
across the bar stirring the memory
of a first kiss?

Some moments we find ourselves
weightless, transparent,
temporarily cast into the iconography
of a St. Michael wielding his sword
or Joan as she succumbed
to the voices that prodded her into battle.
Most times we keep ourselves hungry,
while some of us go on praying,
staunch in our knowing,
that the kingdom of the cross-eyed
will never take over,
cascades of grace
will entomb us as we sleep,

enshrine us in a landscape
sheared of cynicism,
flowering with portents
assuring us, we breathe
as Wender's angels do:
infinite, limitless,
sewn into a pattern of destiny
that matters.

My Roman Spring

1.

The world curtsies as it should tonight.
A Panavision camera scans
a rocky Italian coastline.
Or is it San Francisco?
Vivian Leigh touches her lips.
A crepe scarf unfastens
from around her shoulder
and blows over a desolate terrain.
A fugacious bouquet of columbines
drops from an overlook,
cello and flute comprise the soundtrack.
I climb the shores in search
of the Hermes fichu
the shredded ribbon that bound together
those cherished blooms.

2.

My mother moves her hands
in and out of a pail of Clorox.
A polka tune chafes over the hallway
and underneath the basement stairs
where my cousin Ellis and I are playing
Peter Pan. Ellis pretends to be Wendy,
who is sewing on my shadow,
placing fingers between my thighs
and down around my crotch.
Even at nine I am the older man,
imploring my consort to:
Pull the seams tighter, harder!
Frankie Yankovic's accordion wails

and we mimic kisses
amid coffee cans filled with nails,
stone cherries suspended in Mason jars.

3.

The strobe lights at the Ice Palace
have been rapidly pulsing
for the last four remixes and Gitty
has stripped down to his daisy bikinis.
A red-haired man with a handlebar moustache
offers both of us one hundred dollars
if he can just lick the sweat from off our necks.
Gitty and the freckled cowboy make off
for the toilet stall,
a remake of *Stairway to Heaven*
showers the crowd. I stretch my hands up
over my head as if to catch the mirrored ball,
my nineteen-year-old body
reflected back in a thousand suns,
perfect for one held breath.

4.

I'm listening to Julie London, my ears
cushioned between a set of headphones
at the Tower Records on the Champs-Élysées.
I close my eyes to imagine a cigar lounge,
a young, unshaven Warren Beatty smiling
at the chanteuse singing *Love For Sale*.
My mouth silently forms the lyric:
Love that's only slightly soiled.
I parody the diva's gestures, stroke
chiffon and hairspray. Down the street,
there are cheap sex booths
and for fifty francs I lean

my torso against a hole cut in the wall.
Imagine again that stubble face,
his eyes, those full lips,
as I thrust into a black, wet void,
only slightly soiled.

5.

There are twelve frozen pierogis floating
in a pot on the stovetop. Just like Mama
I am waiting for the water to boil,
for the cheese-filled pockets to thicken
and spin in the churn. The small pies
will shred if left in too long. I orbit
the iron rim. Swim to the center
of the wet heat. I am trying to be born.
Become seasoned. April in Italy
was a long time ago. The ring thrown
into LaSpezia's fountain. Letters
flushed on a train to Vienna. I know
there is more than lament. Water ripples
with foam. I try to convince myself
that I am still here. I let my wrist
stay near the scalding roil too long.
I scream for the life I have loved
and let go of.

Fakir

Not even sleight of hand
can delude the gatekeeper,
turn loaves of bread into keys,
or churn smoke
over the citadel's trapdoor.

Wander the outskirts.
You'll find solace
in other mendicants,
dreamy poets,
the luminous earth.
Hunger is instructional.

Learn to spell your name
with a ouija planchette.
Dance over mud flats,
sleep in open graves.
Eat dust, dung beetles,
sing the marrow out of your bones.
This will become your story,
the way in,
all that you truly own.

Crèche

These tiny figurines crouched
over the veined, porcelain infant
are mute. Their inky smiles
are slightly awry, their eyes,
slits through which the miracle
birth goes unnoticed.

In my mind, I'm small enough
to be a squatter in their lean-to.
Curled up beside the ox or resting
on the belly of the flea-floured mule,
my head rises with each donkey wheeze,
a cold snout nuzzling my groin.

Inside the lonely barn,
shepherds and turbaned guests
swoon in an opiate dust
as an angel struggles to dislodge
her wing from a rafter.

Amid the stable debris,
the nativity animals turn me
into a salt lick. Ratted and venerable,
they lavish a holy baptism upon me
with their tongues
until I shimmer like ivory,
stir and thrash like a new god.

Cavafy's Bones

Sunk before ever reaching Ithaka,
sodden limbs gather against
the jetty's edge. Jerry-rig
these skeleton parts
into a raft. Sail again.

Troll Cat's Truck Stop

Route 30 is desolate on Tuesday morning.
I drive my brother's yellow Camero
to the rest stop on the edge of Bliss Woods.
I play with the straw in my slurpee,
watch the bearded truckers
with their caps and sunglasses
prowl around the parking lot.
They pull up astride each other and push back
the seats in their cabs, their breathing
lightly fogging their windows.
The radio plays Olivia Newton-John or Queen
and I wonder when I will be able
to shave everyday.
I think about getting the nerve
but instead I wait
and search my eyes,
pretend not to notice
I have grown to be eighty in the passing hour.
I sing the lyrics again to Leo Sayer's
You Make Me Feel Like Dancin'
until a Chevy van pulls up next to mine.
The driver is bobbing his head in rhythm
and when he looks over at me
I think to myself, *Another troll*
and nothing, not the long stretch of road
that meanders past Rock City
or three minutes of forgetting myself,
can turn me back into the kid
who loved to play with Matchbox cars,
who wanted to be Patty Duke's television twin,
or who folded the arms of G.I. Joes,
so tightly around their hard bodies,
their mouths clamped onto each other
until both soldiers surrendered.

The Hula Room
on Highway B

We sit on scalloped barstools
that circle around Miss Vicki
and her lip-synched version of *Skylark*,

your eyes adhere blankly
to a skewed tiki mask or some wisp
of a bending bar boy
as you chew the hard ends
of cloves and black licorice seeds.

Oh to be twenty again,
your words bound in a spray of smoke.

Tongue traces the brine trail
at the edge of my Margarita glass
and I think of your salt sweet kisses,
the ones you toss out
to anyone who might ask.

Saugatuck:
Ode to the Dunes

Don't smell the gardenias, you caution,
wasps are sleeping inside those petals.
So I slip off my sandals
to feel the heat of the sunrays
absorbed into the twilight sand dunes.
Then Michael puts on the long version
of Anita Ward's *Ring My Bell*
and me and Aaron and DeLuys
strip down to our bathing trunks,
clink together plastic champagne flutes
through that silly chorus of *ding a ling a ling.*
No one thinks of stepping on a cocklebur,
cutting their toe on broken glass,
or stumbling drunk into Lake Michigan.
We believe that we're immutable.

When Cher begins to sing *Take Me Home,*
Lance shouts *Diva* into the air and declares:
Nineteen eighty-two is going to be the best year.
We live for the Tabasco sauce remixes,
for backyard barbecue vinyl soul cuts,
for disco danger zone diatribes:
Candi Staton's *Young Hearts Run Free,*
Karen Young's silver like a bullet *Hot Shot,*
Sylvester's *Stars.*

Michael is a deejay at the Spectrum Bar.
The bubble bumpin' bonus beats
of Evelyn Champagne King's *Shame* rip.
When she scats with the lyric,
Mama just don't understand,
we hold our hands up in the air

Gerard Wozek

as though we're dancing
at the Pier in Fire Island.
Flecks of Spanish moss fall
from the crooked swamp trees
like party confetti.
Maybe it's because Indian Summer
has come so late to these parts
(the ash leaves have stayed green too long,
the sweetpeas are still in bloom)
that we are tricked into thinking the winter
will not come this year.
So we imagine the moon, a big mirrored ball,
claw off each other's bikini underwear,
hump on Bee Gees beach blankets,
and let the damp gardenia air swell our lungs.

I swear if Michael plays *I Feel Love* once more
I'll pour a pitcher of daiquiris over him,
but Michael isn't at the turntable,
the automatic swingback arm on the stereo
keeps playing that warped twelve-inch
until I notice there is a skip
at the part when Donna sings:
oooh, it's so good it's so good, it's so good.
Then a muffled voice heaves,
Will someone change that record?
I dig my knuckles deep into the coarse sand
to feel a tiny crust of frost forming,
creeping almost imperceptibly,
under and over our reclining bones.

When you wake up after sleeping

with another man,
you think of breathing,
his measured against your own.
How in the dark, your pulses bleat
a secret code under the sheets.
How you want to keep it holy,
as you move towards his familiar
scent: underarm musk mingling
in the air like the scent of pumpkin
and rhubarb, childhood's forest,
crack of ice pond, a cathedral
of branches moaning. Lick
his salt sweat, clenched hand,
powder pearls on his skin,
nipple ring. You want him
to reach back, offer that winter
grove of trees, the woody sap
sticking to fingers, forgotten wishes
written in snow banks, kiss him
and for a moment, it's there.

Side Show

Jimmy played the Dog Faced Boy.
He wagged and foamed
behind steel bars at the circus.
His unclipped nails, hairy arms, and face,
provided him with gainful employment,
but public ridicule. For years
we'd bring milkbones to the Big Top,
and watch him chew them with relish.
Gawkers would often tease him,
throw spit balls or crumpled sacks
with peanut shells in them.

I sometimes dreamt of Jimmy's escape,
dreamt of his warm dog man body,
dreamt his tail between my legs,
his tongue in my ear,
his teeth on my skin—just hard enough.

One night, I snuck out to unlock his cage,
found Jimmy, curled in a corner,
studied his heavy breathing,
touched his neck,
felt my pulse rise,
felt myself harden,
then the dog eyes opened,
his nostrils flared with my scent,
our instincts began to meld.

Jimmy on all fours.
Jimmy, my Dog Faced Boy.
Jimmy, my master.

Manifest

We swallow silk
and become enlightened.
What is left for us to do now?
Somnambulant, you stare
up at the preview video
in the quarter slot show booth.

I like the torso shots, you say,
chewing through your cigarette butt.
The smooth thrusts,
the way his hair blows in the wind.

Your clef chin is dripping
with my raw honey.
Careful, I say.
Your eyes give back
my whole desire
to be absolved from past sins,
sweetly held in the palm of God,
as whenever Mahalia sings.

At the end of the film
is a cautionary warning
about condoms.
You shut it out. Become
the lily turning on water.
You say, *Our skin is humming pore to pore.*
I say, *Body remember bliss.*

Remember to trust this pulse, this sweat,
this intent to merge and make manifest
the urging of our senses.

Gerard Wozek

We hold each to each,
enveloped in the center,
spinning lotus petals of kisses
that keep us safe.

Spell for Changing Bodies

Some lure takes hold,
unshakable pattern
of chords, then bluster,
salt wave, Eros turning
tiny hairs to fire.

Cure of lips, hands,
let it be irreversible,
let gooseflesh, tumult.
Let burst of cornflower,
let opening utterly.

If touch breaks stone
clavicle down to blood
red flame, unfetters
grief, know your heart
as honeycomb, leaf
palace, sea grove.

Let stroke of fingertips,
let barkshield crumble,
let dismantling completely.

Be inhabited, be Jove
arriving, imprint on skin
becoming song, perfect
melody lingering.

Pilgrimage

1.

At Père Lachaise

Tourists at this cemetery
have moved on to scan
the epitaphs of Marcel Proust,
Sarah Bernhardt. Leave plastic
lilies on the grave of Gertrude Stein,
wend hippie beads around a bust
of Jim Morrison. Near the marble
homage to holocaust victims,
men in black leather and military
attire, lean on altar rails.
Half-exposed in the thresholds
of open mausoleums, they orgy
in the ransacked graves of erased
heroes, financiers, patron saints.
A teenager in a French navy uniform
shoots over a sparse wreath holder,
the dead poinsettia leaves
clinging to the thin frame tremble,
come to life with white dew.

2.

Off the Pont Neuf

Edith Piaf is piped in
at La Samaritaine where
tourists hoard felt berets,
Toulouse Lautrec dishtowels,
beltbuckles shaped

like the Arc de Triomphe.
Where are the salons
of Madame de Sevigne
and Moliere? Haunts
of Proust and Cocteau?
Off Rue de Rivoli, past
keychain and postcard vendors,
is the Hammam St. Paul:
Oscar Wilde in steam,
la vie en rose.

3.

At the Rue de Casablanca

I sing praises to my destroyer,
to the Shiva who harangues me,
to the faceless river god,
captain of the Bateau Mouche,
to the loaded revolver waiting
behind a carton of shredded wheat,
to Queen Insomnia who throws
the syllables of my name around,
to the rabid lust that animates me
like a mute sock puppet,
to the ishkabibble who begs
for my penny loafers,
to the gray Atlantic that will cover
my bones at St. Michel,
to psalms remembered from Sunday school,
promises of a *Balm in Gilead,*
to incessant drumbeats,
zombie rhythm at boy clubs,
to the fat puttis and gargoyles
that hover over me,
to Paris angels
wherever I may meet them.

4.

Near the Jardin de Flore

Why do you stay in France?
My passport has been stolen.
Are your clothes off yet?
My hands are sticky from the riz au lait.
Do you consider yourself lucky?
I jump over turnstiles without getting caught.
Is this smoke bothering your eyes
Don't worry, these aren't tears.
Have you thought about working in films?
I can tilt my cap like Brando did.
Think of me as more than a friend?
I've a ticket for a train to Amsterdam.
Is this your idea of whimsy?
I lost my Plan du Paris, I just wander.
Can you sleep on top of me?
Do you know the story of Pierrot Le Fou?
Is it alright if we don't talk?
Remember me if you want, I won't write.

5.

Taxi to Charles DeGaulle Airport

I know these French streets,
this bend in the river, winter
frost gripping cobbled paths,
gutted clock tower, fenced-in
cluster of park benches.
On the Rue des Rosiers,
I danced with haloed poets,
shimmied for diplomats
at the Ritz, a motorcycle crew
near the Place de la Concorde,

a yogurt maker from Rimes.
At the Bastille, I spoke
my confessions to an Algerian
barber. He cut my hair, I jostled
his shaved scrotum on my tongue.
Here is where I lived
on butterscotch tea, crème brûlée.
Mute as snow, I climbed
the Mount of Mercury,
to kiss a Moroccan crepe vender,
genuflected in St. Chappelle
before a dodgy priest,
twirled through Pigalle to lose
my fortune to a gypsy. I take back
no snapshots of the Eiffel Tower,
no postcards from the Louvre.
My hands fold shut this map
of skins. I do no penance
for tempting celestial bodies.
I burn with Rimbaud's fire.
I pray to those who have forfeited
the sky, this rarefied air. I kneel
in remembrance of seraphs.

Dervish

Sometimes I wish I were you,
those crooked labyrinths
of the Medina you saunter through,
the scent of hashish and mint leaves
drying the Moroccan sun.
African musk burns off your neck
as you pass bundled women
slumped behind umbrella stalls,
heaped over with bruised
persimmons, figs, cedar shavings.

The portal to ecstasy opens
with the curvy bend
of your lips as you greet strangers
in the ville nouvelle. Tourists,
heady from the balm or drunk
from the altitudes, swoon in your heat.
What is that charm dangling
at your clavicle that gilds you,
makes you a god?

Greeted at the taverna
with a round of champagne splits,
moustached kisses, caresses
from muscle-hard arms,
drumbeats sift you onto the floor,
wing your feet like Mercury's.
Dancers pulse toward you
to shower in your frenzied sweat.
Someone passes a fez cap
filled with cocaine. The room blurs,
your nose and lips, inflamed with fire.

If I could be anything
I would be the impulse
that moves through you,
the urge that sends your body
tumbling as though you were yoked
onto a windmill, the kif-flushed
blood that curls through your veins,
the dense core that centers you
as you swallow the scorpions,
coax the cobras to dance,
spin into emptiness, align
with the planets, become
the threshold to all-knowing.

Let me taste the plum
nights of your open palm,
hold the memory of all the boys
who've orbited around you,
pining to touch your lips,
steady your axis. Let me be
what encircles your flung
open arms. The reed pipe
that whirrs you into prayer,
the newborn earth in trance,
the mad, insatiable turning,
as you enter
the eye of your God.

Vienna

1.

Café Society

Isn't that what we want? Not the jolt
from a mélange at the Hawelka or the gnashing
of caffeine teeth over gossip, the hyper-reality
offered by a sacretorte. Bells peal
for fifteen straight minutes over Stephansplatz.
Grace lunging at us from every carved deity.
In the courtyard outside Café Ball,
we loosen our coats, unbutton collars, and feel
our chests pressed hotly to one another,
rising steadily, each breath centered
on something intangible, as if at any moment
we could be absorbed into
this sudden, undoubtable silence.

2.

At the Jewish Cemetery

No waltzes here. We stumble over rubble,
toppled onyx, and coal marble scattered
on the tall grass paths. The pall of time's
verdigris, a shroud over untended graves:
Stein, Rosenberg, Schiller.
Where are the families who will light
candles on the granite,
the caretakers who will sweep
the mausoleums, the mourners
who will pray Kaddish? You pull at ivy
wending through a cracked headstone. Blood

leaves grown over the chiseled name. Wordless,
we have no sense that a violet is opening,
some new music being born.

3.

At Sisi's Hermesvilla

How much we want to fit into her slippers, glide
organdy chenille, brushed silk over our toes,
feel the instep tufted with doe's fur.
But the guide tells us they were never worn,
just like the hooded trundle bed, pristine
in a room painted with Titania's lace
and winged feys. Faust in stone brooding
over an unopened grimoire. Love spells.
All of her majesty's
personal effects are roped off,
encased under glass, enchantment's artifice
lit for gapers. We try to imagine her hand
on the circular fan with marabou feathers,
or the peacock quills where
the great Kaiser Elizabeth, recluse, poet,
would compose her verses
to the *Souls of the Future,*
inventing a dynasty to be inhabited
by Ariel, King Cup, and us.

4.

At the Kunsthistorische

I count the pearl crane heads ringing
the toes of Isis, while your whiskers chisel
at my torso. A museum guard dozes
through our pantomime, your mouth
divining fire beneath this sculpted stone.

5.

From Schoenbrunn Gardens

You cup the last blooms into your hand,
noting each name: Peer Gynt, Sutter's Gold,
Apogee, Elektra. *I'll dry these at home*, you say,
use them for an infusion or a charm.
School kids go giddy down the park slides,
oblivious to sculpted hedges,
dying bougainvillea, art nouveau
lattice caving in on the greenhouses.
Gripped by bales of laughter,
they are suspended in a spell
of giggles, given the key to inhabit
heaven's spark, claim this Eden.
Take nothing away.

6.

Demmer's Tee Haus

Nowhere but here do we find
edgeless white bread smeared
with fish roe, wrought-iron baskets
with globs of candied oranges, nutmeg,
clove spears, winter pudding,
plaid-ribboned fudge.
I offer you the marzipan swan.
You take its neck
in your mouth and bite down.
Let it steep here: darjeeling,
vanilla bourbon, oolong Formosa.
It's not the brew we've come for,
but the gentility. Royal-crested porcelain
and embroidered cozies, baby spoons grazing
sugar cellars. On a placemat is a sketch

of two Burmese soldiers stooping
to sip over a broken tea crate.
Names of exotic herb blends ring
the paper cartouche.
I note the exaggerated padding
in the shoulders of their uniforms,
how they're leaning together so close.
Still separate. The distant world
held in their cups, evaporating.

Gellert Hotel Sauna

Sage vapors engulf
the men of Budapest.
At this hammam,
working class gents
soak and sweat next
to the terry toweled
elite, lose themselves
in smoke, heal bruises
in medicine waters.
Eucalyptus oil for rubbing
out stiffness, citrus
for grief. Tears
are cool puddles left
on long wooden slats.
The muscular and rotund
shower and stretch.
Equalized in the jungle
humidity, they find a balm
to polish vertebrae,
thighs, clavicles. Come
chanting Bacchus heat,
seek the succor of spray,
discover omnipotence
in the swirling pools.

At Sitges

Sperm and death leak out
of subterranean caves
where tribes once gathered for meals.
A splayed watermelon over
the unopened condom, you swallow
the seeds for luck.

Song for Distingue Lovers

No kisses tonight. Just chins
heavy on folded pillows.

Bodies sick to death of sheets
over mattress ruts.

Her voice wavers,
I wonder where our love has gone.

And you think of birdsong
trilling over pastis glasses,

tingle of legs barely
touching under café tables.

The first time you really heard
Billie sing.

A Calendar from Krakow

with unpronounceable days.
Printed with glossy photos
of floodlit church steeples
and crenellated towers.
Exotica to pitch
a tourist's imagination elsewhere.
The camera lens keeps
less affluent residents
out of the frame.
Perhaps they're behind
the old cloth hall
or in the pee-rancid train depot
where the old communist songs
still raise the rafters.
Wood shavings on the waiting room
floor make soft nests
at the shoeless feet of comrades,
where their carved birds
wait to fly overseas
for only two zloty.

Lucia di Lammermoor

Of course we have come
to see her go mad.
Craning our necks from the balcony
to see the first twinkle of her sweat,
faery dew sparking over the aria.
The libretto stirs Lucia toward panic,
then a palpable terror,
twitching under her skin
like a pinched nerve.
By the second act,
she's a wounded sparrow.
We're giddy from her coloratura,
insane flute notes lodged in her hair,
blood, a gargle in her throat.
As the diva gathers momentum,
we prolong our clapping as if to say:
Self-destruct Lucy. Kill yourself!
Offstage, our heroine withers,
then the curtain comes down
on her beloved's suicide.
We bruise our fingers in the dark,
cry out, *Brava! Encore!*
For our own final act,
for the bird once crushed,
by our own hands.

Le Mal du Pays

A man in a Magritte suit,
black wings hung
on stooped shoulders,
leans over the railing of a bridge,
combed hair, featureless face.
He scans a Paris skyline
obscured by clouds.

Beside him rests a docile lion
who squelches his jungle instinct.
The motionless King of Beasts
contemplates the fabrication
of ringed human hands,
the scent of perfumed skin.

What Gabriel would stall
with wings the color of soot?
What is this homesickness
in his bent posture?
Why doesn't the lion pounce?
Why doesn't the angel soar?
What tames them to the ground?

Tiger's Eye

I still have it,
that moss-caked tile,
verdigris scorched to a glowing copper,
from our holiday in the Cinqueterre.
Remember how your fingers moved
over the chipped patina
of that Byzantine mosaic,
the one that faced the jet spraying Pan?
You denounced the inflated lire
as your sunburned hand grazed
the neck of stippled tiger
suspended over Dante's fire pit.
As you reached towards the ocular region
of that tiled masterpiece,
a half-lapis, half-opal square dislodged
and stuck to your moist open palm.
You've plucked out his eye!
The astonishment in my voice halted a tourist
from sipping her espresso in the adjacent plaza.

Later that night,
two *malfortuna* beans
(instead of the blessings of three)
floated in our walnut-cloudy Sambucas
as we bickered over
the vocal range of Mirella Freni,
how I'd change my train ticket home.
You held the eye in your hand,
intimate and iridescent,
and tried to rub ten thousand years
of Peloponnesian war dross
out of that cat's cornea.

Today I read the postcard you've sent

from our favorite pension in LaSpezia:
*They've replaced the dun shutters
in the Northern villa*, you write,
You'd hardly recognize the islands.
I imagine you taking your lover's hand
as you stroll the rim of the cypress grottos
or lifting an amber-veined wineglass
to the piazza's imperishable fountain
where a blind feline,
charred, corroded in ash,
tries to paw himself out of the red coal abyss.

Daylight

Something like clouds assemble,
fog banked at the crook of my elbow,
vapor blanketing my skin.

No mouth to wake me,
lips to melt spine,
invocation of whispers: *Deeper, deeper.*

Somewhere crows carry dawn in,
a black wing cathedral
over the thighs of iconic lovers,
entwined limbs turning to petals.

Nowhere, here,
scent of your vetiver,
our knotted fingers, coil of sweat.

Nettles of gray light inch over bed sheets,
my skin turning to shale leaf,
then granite, a bloodless
statue needing your hands,

the psalm of our soft moans,
gathering and breaking
like morning.

Elk Song

Empty of wisdom,
I call in elk,
using an ancient
chief's medicine
bundle. Astonished,
they stride
into my loft, heavy
hooves, nostrils
flared, tails ratted
with cockleburs,
beer can tops.
They cower
at jackhammers,
sirens, nestle under
glass coffee tables,
chew out stuffing
from my Bauhaus sofa.
I try to calm them,
imitate a cricket,
sway like a mountain
pine. Unappeased,
they stall in my kitchen.
What chant will reverse
the spell, point them
home, turn them toward
alpine paths? If they leave
on their own, sure
of the fenceless prairies,
Queen Anne's lace,
I'll go with them,
trusting that their path
is the right one.

Ritual for Letting Go

Place your ear on the thick trunk of a tree,
listen for the sap rising at its core,
note any bird song laced on the oakwind.

You must be wild.
You must persist.

Run until you are breathless
then smudge your face with leaves and mud,
hold your heaving chest and wait
until your unleashed sobs relent.
Write his name and place it in a packet,
a sacred pouch you have prepared.

Think about the mossy beach in Ireland
where you hunted for coral together,
the canyon where you kept vigil
over his persistent fever.

Take the pouch and hang it
on a tree branch.
Recall the way his arms
grew into sparrow wings,
so thin, so frail, you were afraid
to even hold him.

Whirl your body around in circles,
kiss the wind, the rough tree bark.
Remember the tremor of sap rising in him,
in you, in your throat,
as you sing his name to the sky.

Rumi

When you say, *Beloved,* remember:

setting free cotton from milkweed pods,
the coasting of geese making for heat,
breath on the mirror, your name
traced in the fog, present
for a moment.

Heaven of the Fixed Stars

When will the sand speak
to me again:
hush haven hush.

When will clouds be clouds
and the wind shirr my body
into music? (The looked over
driftwood whispers:
it is always so.)

Your moccasins flung next to mine,
radio static over storm reports,
sweat damp bedsheets,
the Santa Ana drying the roof
of my mouth, still
your urgent kisses, then
sleep soundless sleep.

Spirits blanket the desert basin,
spark in and out of bodies,
move through rocks, water,
rolling shrubs. Moon wanes
from fullness to suffuse with the dark.
What disappears from view
is never really gone.

Steady hand gently pulls
the bedsheet over my shoulder,
dream dancing dream.
It is always so.

Troubadours of Fire

How many pesos should I toss
to the fearless boys? The honey-skinned
brujos at the plaza intersection
shrieking flames into twilight air.

How can they risk placing so many
oil soaked wands down their throats,
blowing into the sky with such fervid notes?
Nipples dart, sweat-slick chests reflect
the dance of the blaze.

You say on the cracked calles
of Mexico City, it is better to breathe fire
than the rank air itself,
trapped exhaust fumes
mingling with burnt grease
from crumbling paella parlors.

I see the curving neon signature
of the Coca-Cola billboard
as it beams over the quiet paseos,
caved-in shopping malls. I know
the silent spark in eyes at the Zócalo,
nervous hand jobs in parking lot
stairwells, tongue kisses
over the top of bathroom stalls.

But oh, to be one of the brazen,
shooting sparks into the open air,
showering native pedestrian,
dumb-struck tourist with dreadless
rhapsodies of El Diablo. I fold

a ten-thousand peso note
into one outstretched hand
and my blackest nightmare
is sung to ash.

Confessing Sins

Who will absolve me from all my desertions,
aborted affairs, treasons of flesh?

Did I love them enough before parting,
waltzing skin to skin,
a momentary circle of solace?

Who can forgive me now, bless me,
for have I sinned through my half-mumbled
endearments, wrong numbers scribbled
on matchbooks, spurious abandonments
at the Motel 6?

Unable to surrender to the body
that slept next to me, the real force
lay hidden, untapped, pulsing inside me,
vital as air, promising to take on a new form:

two planets fusing into one
or a coiled uroborous snake,

not this fearsome, predatory bird
rising higher and higher
over bodies licked to ash.

Ice Elegy (after Takamura Kotaro)

Put snow on my lips,
you said, *I'm brushfire*.
So I wrapped an ice cube
into tissue and pressed winter
to your whiskers.
A cold trickle down your neck
quaked you for a moment
out of fever delirium.
You slid into the Tundra
of your boyhood,
and the silver lozenge sled,
the frozen pond
where you used to skate,
all came back.
You let out a great sigh
as you waved at yourself,
childhood's blue scarf, a blur,
as you sped headfirst
into white December hills.

The Berdache's Kiss

You enter his tent. Firelight guides you
through dark folds of hanging
animal skins, beaded cloth,
until you stand at the center,
a stone-marked medicine wheel.

All directions emanate from you
as you're carefully sponged down
with clover oil and warm flower jelly.

Attention is lavished upon
your feet and genitals,
buttocks and face,
as the smoke from a sage wand
chafes your naked body clean.

A spiral dance of feathered bodies
has roped around the tent,
setting our names free
in the drum flecked air:

water dancer
cloud charmer
talons of the invisible ones
medicine of the warrior.

When the tremors have passed
through your painted body
and you wake in your own small bed,
you press your fingers to your lips,
remembering, it is his devotion
that keeps you strong.

Gerard Wozek

Say Goodbye

to the world. You can do this.
Put your hands over your eyes
and don't peek. Now feel
the darkness rushing in
over your still warm pulse.
Go ahead. Take in a breath
and hold it. For the last time
remember leaves, the way the grass
browns in the hottest part of August,
then the summoning of birds
to distant places. Remember what held you
the first time you saw the Rift Valley
or knelt before a mosque.
Let go of this: horizon and sky,
this pockmarked planet
with its armaments. Let sand
cover up the famines and machinery,
the refugee camps, the neon theme parks.
Let the continents break in two
swallowing all of your beautiful pictures:
your trip to Zambia,
the moon over the desert.
Go on, let it happen.
You won't wake up now
to feel the bruises of your childhood,
the gasp that floats in your belly
every time you look at a calendar.
Allow the temperate zones to merge
so that only the spin, the crazy whirl,
embraces you. Sink into mercy.
Wait here in this in between,
in this no-time. In creation's bed.
Whatever you believe will enclose you.
This darkness is replaced by something
more solemn, holier

than your first prayerbook,
but as familiar as a handshake,
the parting of friends, a kiss.

Shaman

1.

I won't let them bury me. I am a slow
deliberate gait, frenzied dance.
I inhale their ghost breath, take in
their flesh stench, untangle memories
from their hair. I keep awake.

2.

I take unthinkable risks. I stoop
to catch their dew.
Lick the dust from stone lips.
In their dreams I flower, shoot open
warm petals, let my stamen ooze through.
They eat my seeds and live again.

3.

I love, some say, too ardently.
I suck the poison from their bruised veins.
I grow strong.

4.

I am the Magus at the crossroads,
Berdache at the produce stand,
flaming fagus branch, Prince of Wands.
I am Winkte and Nadle.
Angakok and Poha-kant. Pansy

on the Tennessee mountain path,
bedouin in the sand. I am the sought after
oracle, warrior, double-spirit.

5.

I live between two worlds. I am
everywhere and nowhere. Some try
to say my name, erase it,
bury my truth. I persist.

The Nature Sonnets by Jill Williams
> 1st edition, ISBN 1-928589-10-3, $8.95
>
> An innovative collection of sonnets that speaks to the cycle of nature and life, crafted with wit and clarity.
>
> "...Refreshing and pleasing."
>
> — Miles David Moore, author of *The Bears of Paris*

Recuerdos by Robert L. Giron
> 1st edition, in Spanish, ISBN 1-928589-03-0, $4.95
>
> A chapbook in Spanish of a maternal grandfather's life and adventure in the Greater Southwest of the United States.

Songs for the Spirit by Robert L. Giron
> 1st edition, ISBN 1-928589-08-1, $16.95
>
> A philosophical work in verse which reflects a vision of the new millennium, with a feminist twist, filled with the Spirit.
>
> "This is an extraordinary book."
>
> — John Shelby Spong, author of *Why Christianity Must Change or Die: A Bishop Speaks to Believers in Exile*

Wrestling with Wood by Robert L. Giron
> 3rd edition, ISBN 1-928589-05-7, $5.95
>
> A chapbook of impressionist moods and feelings of a long-term relationship which ended in a tragic death.
>
> "...nuggets of truth and beauty sprout within our souls."
>
> — Teresa Bevin, author of *Havana Split*

For Book Orders Only, Call: 800.247.6553
Or Write: Gival Press, LLC / PO Box 3812 / Arlington, VA 22203
Or Visit: givalpress.com

Books Available from Gival Press

Dervish by Gerard Wozek

    1st edition, ISBN 1-928589-11-1, $15.00

    Winner of the 2000 Gival Press Poetry Contest. This rich whirl of the dervish traverses a grand expanse from bars to crazy dreams to fruition of desire.

    "...By Jove, these poems shimmer."

    — Gerry Gomez Pearlberg, author of *Mr. Bluebird*

Dreams and Other Ailments — Sueños y otros achaques by Teresa Bevin

    1st edition, in English & Spanish, ISBN 1-928589-13-8, $21.00

    A wonderful array of short stories about the fantasy of life and tragedy but filled with humor and hope.

    "...*Dreams and Other Ailments* will lift your spirits...."

    — Dr. Lynne Greeley, Critic & Professor of Theatre, University of Vermont

Flint Shards from Sussex by Jeff Man

    1st edition, ISBN 1-928589-12-X, $8.95

    Winner of the 1999 Gival Press Poetry Contest. Passion and love are invoked in this marvelous collection of poetry loosely based on *Wuthering Heights*.

    "...a book of lyric intensity..." — Diane Wakoski, author of *Argonaut Rose*

    "A poignant collection." — Katherine Soniat, author of *A Shared Life*

Impressions Françaises by Robert L. Giron

    2nd edition, in French, ISBN 1-928589-06-5, $4.95

    Haiku about historical events and people of France.

    "A beautiful and moving homage to the land of [his] ancestors."

    — President Jacques Chirac

Metamorphosis of the Serpent God by Robert L. Giron

    1st edition, ISBN 1-928589-07-3, $12.00

    A collection of poetic forms which embrace the past and the present, ethnic and sexual identity, the mystical and the personal.